THE FIFTH WA\

Zombie – the extinction of man dream

It is June 3, 2021, and my body is in stress right now. I went to my dad's yesterday. Did his laundry and cleaned a bit. Took him to do his blood test and now I am home. Well, been home for a bit. Fell asleep in the late afternoon and my daughter brought me the phone. He called and woke me out of my deep sleep. Waking, I thought it was the next day because it was so lit outside. Could not speak to him, and I went back to sleep, and now my body is in distress.

Did I meet someone this morning coming back home after getting breakfast?

Yes, but I was not interested. He was okay looking, and he sounded African. I wanted to ask him his lineage, but I did not.

He was driving by and saw me at the bus stop and stopped his 4x4 to speak to me. He thought me good looking, but I was not biting.

He offered me a lift and I politely declined. He also wanted my phone number, but I told him no. I was not interested. Leaving he said, *"we will see each other again."* I said to myself; I doubt that.

Wow. Now you are up to date on my happenings but not fully. Before going to sleep while lying in bed, *I COULD FEEL THE EARTH VIBRATING.* It was so strong that it was scary for me. The vibration did not last for a second, it lasted for a while. Thus, me falling asleep again without knowing when I feel asleep.

I have never felt so scared while feeling Mother Earth vibrating before. It's a DEAR GOD FEELING BECAUSE; I TRULY DO NOT KNOW WHEN *MOTHER EARTH IS GOING TO UNLEASH HER FURY HERE IN CANADA EARTHQUAKE WISE.*

So yes, disaster is going to hit Canada and this I know, but to feel the Earth; Mother Earth vibrating in such a way is scary. Therefore, I truly do not know the consequences of her actions and or, what the consequences catastrophe wise here in Canada is going to be.

I will not worry about it. I cannot worry about it. Major things are going to happen to Canada, and Canadians cannot blame anyone but Canadians – well, *THE DIFFERENT GOVERNMENTS OF CANADA.*

White People have to pay for their crimes historically as well as, the crimes they are doing today. Yes, it's sad that we cannot live in true peace, but this is not God's fault; it is our fault as humans. We spread hate, teach hate, push hate, and more. Sad yes, but this is people globally. I do not know what living in hate and dysfunction solve.

Why hate each other when you know the outcome of your hate is Death?

You spreading hate is not the answer to life. And none of you say, I should not talk considering the way I cuss out White People in these books. And I will tell you again from some of my other books.

"I DO NOT HAVE TIME TO WASTE HATING WHITE PEOPLE. MY LIFE IS TOO PRECIOUS TO HATE; WHITE PEOPLE."

I refuse to hate White People. I am better than that. Yes, cuss dem out reckless an rude I will do, *but I refuse to hate them.* I know hell. Therefore, I know the hell that some must face once the spirit shed the flesh.

"HELL IS THE VICTORY OF AND OR, FOR LIFE." Therefore, Death protects all who are good and true by ensuring *"NO ONE WICKED AND EVIL HATH LIFE, OR CAN ATTAIN SPIRITUAL LIFE WITH GOD."*

So yes, given the actions of White People they've sacrificed self to and or, unto Death.

White People cannot and will never escape their hell. This I know for a fact without doubt. Therefore, they; Whites; the White Race too must learn and know the consequences of their lies and actions; murderous tendencies globally.

Just as Whites are guilty of Genocide, we as Blacks are guilty also. We refuse to wake up and unite truthfully for the better good of Blacks globally.

We refuse to live right. Thus, we've become confused fighting to be included in systems that don't give a damn about us.

Listen, these books are not meant to spread hate, and I refuse anyone who use these books to spread hate. Lovey and Death know what to do to anyone who use these books to spread hate, teach hate, or hate anyone. No, I refuse to be like Death's Children and People that give you lies and hate. God do not put strife in the heart or hearts of anyone. *WE AS HUMANS FUEL STRIFE AND HATE.*

WE AS HUMANS CONDITION OTHERS TO HATE.

WE AS HUMANS PUT HATE AND STRIFE IN THE HEART AND MIND OF OTHERS.

WE AS HUMANS TEACH HATE.
WE AS HUMANS BREED HATE.
WE AS HUMANS SPREAD HATE.

I refuse to breed hate, spread hate, tell you or anyone to hate another nation because it is plain out wrong.

I truly don't want it for myself so why the hell would I want it for someone else.

No, I truly don't care if you think I am a racist. That's your opinion and feel of me. As long as God shield all who read these books from hate, I am truly blessed and more than good to go.

My truth for God; Lovey is more than unconditional therefore, I will walk in my truth with God.

God never said Michelle, spread hate.
God never said Michelle, teach hate.

God never said Michelle, fuel hate in the different nations.

God never said Michelle, I hate land X or Y.

God never said Michelle, I hate the different races.

God never said Michelle, do all that is wrong to the different nations, including our people. So no, I refuse to hate the different nations. It is not worth it, and my god is too precious to me for me to lose Lovey.

Yes, I've said I've loathe, and hate in other books but; I refuse to tell anyone to hate another human being or nation. I categorically refuse to.

It's not just Whites who are guilty of Sin. We as Black People are guilty of Sin also.

Hell no, I truly do not want or need to see the faces of demons. There is enough demons living and walking amongst us here on Earth and, although some of you think they are good looking, nice, sweet, you have not seen the darkness – their sin and sins around them and on them therefore, I see it, and know it.

Why the hell should I walk in death when I can have life with Lovey good and true continually day in and day out without end?

Now after he woke me up and going back to sleep thus causing my physical body stress and distress. My dreams scared the crap out of me. Therefore, something is truly not right.

Dreamt, I was somewhere, and this white couple; family was in their vehicle. I do not know if they were broken down, but they were in their vehicle. I would say they were on vacation. It was nighttime. All I saw was 3 males in Polynesian Attire who had spears. I am not sure if it's feather or bamboo that was on them as a part of their attire. I know there was some yellow in their attire and they were dark skinned.

The three men went on a feeding frenzy by grabbing the lady and biting her. Like a Zombie would from a Zombie Movie. Yes, the blood and gore. She did not survive and the husband there was no escape for him. In the dream I wondered about their kids.

After that, I was somewhere else. People were hiding under ground, and this young man went to get water, and he scooped some up in his hand where metal covered the area. Think drain covering but with metal and or, think grades steel reinforcement as a covering. I got scared and said to myself about the Zombie's getting him, and sure enough wow. Zombies got him.

After all that, did I see Black People dying?

Yes, Black People were dying. Therefore, Black People are going to be eradicated on a mass scale.

You know what the horrible part is of seeing Black People dying is; _THE RESONANCE OF UNITY._

In the dream, IT RESONATED THAT WE LACK UNITY. So, _because Blacks lack unity and true unity, Blacks are going to die on a mass scale._

I will not take away from this resonance because; _BLACK PEOPLE ARE TRULY NOT UNIFIED._

WE DO NOT COME TOGETHER TRUTHFULLY AND HELP EACH OTHER. WE ARE LIKE ONTO CRABS IN A BARREL THAT TEAR EACH OTHER; THE ENTIRE BLACK RACE DOWN. Therefore, we need to start changing self.

We build other nations and refuse to build us good and true.

SO YES, _OUR LACK OF UNITY IS ALSO WHAT'S GOING TO KILL US._ And rightfully so because wi too fool fool.

Instead of keeping our wealth and helping each other viably, we squander it all thus, other nations has and have raped Black Nations of it all. Africa, and the theft of Africa's Wealth is a prime example.

The Caribbean is also another prime example.

So no, *THE DEATH OF BLACKS IS DUE TO BLACKS. WE REFUSE TO LISTEN TO GOOD AND TRUE ADVICE.*

WE REFUSE TO BUILD OUR BLACK NATIONS.

WE REFUSE TO BUILD EACH OTHER.

WE REFUSE TO UNITE TRUTHFULLY WITH EACH OTHER.

Listen, WE REFUSED OUR OWN BLACK GOD THEREFORE, BLACKS HAVE NO ONE TO BLAME FOR THE DEMISE OF BLACKS APART FROM BLACKS PERIOD.

<u>WE AS BLACKS GAVE UP OUR BLACK GOD TO BECOME MASCOTS GLOBALLY FOR THE DIFFERENT RACES; NATIONS.</u>

Now time is winding down for the different races and STILL BLACK PEOPLE CANNOT COME TOGETHER COLLECTIVELY AND UNITE POSITIVELY FOR THE BETTER GOOD OF BLACKS GLOBALLY.

Death; THE CHILDREN AND PEOPLE OF DEATH DID DO THEIR JOBS. NOW HUMANITY MUST PAY THE PRICE FOR THEIR SINS.

As for Russia, I cannot tell you what is going to happen in that region. I saw dirt and or, wet dirt. You can say mud. I will not analyze this dream because it is not for me to analyze. White People have to be; must be held accountable for their sins. They cannot get away with the ills they've done to the different nations from then until now including tomorrow.

<u>Yes, God need someone to be saved in that land; Russia. Someone need to get themself and his family the hell out of Russia, and I am so going</u>

to leave this alone because I've said enough already.

And no, I will not beg Lovey or Mother Earth for Black People. Black People must stand on their own ground now. We are the ones to continually reject God.

We are the ones that continually believe and trust in the lies of the Bible of Man.

We are the ones as Black People to accept the nastiness the White Race gave us to accept for a God.

We as Black People are the ones to deny God our truth and rights.

We as Black People are the ones to deny us our own God of truth.

We as Black People are the ones to deny God our thanks for the blessings God has and have blessed us with.

God did show us the right and true way. We are the ones to deny the right and true way God has and have given us for all that is nasty; unclean.

As Black People, we fail to realize that when we accept all that is nasty and unclean, we become unclean.

We marry unclean.
We die unclean.
We procreate unclean.
We live unclean.

We hand down all that is nasty and unclean to our children, and future generations.

We also forfeit God – THE TRUE AND LIVING GOD when we accept all that is nasty and unclean.

Yes, I am thinking of God, Mother Earth, and Marcus Mosiah Garvey. All tried to help us as Black People and all Blacks has and done is help to destroy them. So no, I will not pray for Black People or petition God, Mother Earth, or anyone to PROTECT ALL IN THE BLACK RACE. I will however petition God, and Mother Earth for the safety and protection of the GOOD AND TRUE, AND THE TRULY TRYING TO BE GOOD ONLY.

IT SHOULD NOT HAVE TO TAKE ME TO DREAM THE MASS DEATH AND OR,

EXTINCTION OF BLACKS WITH OUR LACK OF UNITY RESONATING SO CLEARLY FOR US TO SEE JUST HOW UNUNITED WE ARE AS A RACE AND PEOPLE.

How many over the years have and has told us we need to unite?

How many songs are out there stressing the unification of Blacks? Now I am dreaming about our lack of unification.

WE AS BLACK PEOPLE NEED TO WAKE UP BECAUSE YOU ARE BEING TOLD IN DEATH THAT BLACKS LACK UNITY. WE NEED TO UNITE FOR THE GOOD AND TRUE GOOD OF ALL BLACKS GLOBALLY.

THIS IS OUR WAKEUP CALL – FINAL CALL FOR US TO UNITE. WE HAVE TO DO BETTER FOR US COME ON NOW. Earth is changing and it is going to get worse. Once worse comes, WHERE WILL BLACK PEOPLE BE?

DO YOU THINK YOU AS BLACKS WILL BE AT THE TOP OF THE FOOD CHAIN OF SAVING WHEN DESTRUCTION FULLY HIT EARTH SHORTLY?

THINK, AND BE WISE.

Come together and start praying good and true to God for whom I call Lovey.

Ask God to protect you collectively.

God cannot save us if God do not know us.

God cannot help us, if we are not of Life; God.

Seek forgiveness from God for hurting God come on now. Many things you truly did not know, and still do not know.

WE ARE GOING TO DIE. THEREFORE, PRESERVE YOUR LIFE IN GOD AND WITH GOD TRUTHFULLY. YOU HAVE MY DREAM OF WHAT I SEE AND KNOW. WAKE UP AND LET'S UNITE GOOD AND TRUE, POSITIVE; SO THAT

GOD CAN FIND FAVOUR IN US AND SAVE US.

YOU, INCLUDING THE YOUNGER GENERATION OF KIDS THAT ARE IN WARM LANDS, START PLANTING FOOD. STOP SITTING BY THE ROAD CORNER, STOP HANGING OUT WITH FRIENDS, STOP DOING THE ILLS OF THE DIFFERENT GANGS, START BEING PRODUCTIVE FOOD AND WATER WISE. HARVEST RAINWATER FROM NOW. START PLANTING YOUR LITTLE VEGETABLES AND FRUITS AND TALK TO GOD TO KEEP YOUR CROPS SAFE AND SECURE FROM THIEVES.

As Black People we need to be self reliant. We cannot depend on our Black Leaders or any Leader to protect us or help us.

We as a People individually and collectively have to come together and start saving us as a Race and People.

We have to depend on self.
We have to help self.
We have to help each other.

To the different Black Organizations out there.
It's time to prepare, start stocking up to help your
Black Own shortly.

To those that will now listen to good and true
counsel. NEVER STOP TALKING TO GOD
YOUR WAY SO THAT GOD CAN PROTECT
YOU AND SAVE YOU.

Never forget, GOD GIVE A LITTLE. Yes, it's little
by little with God.

START DOING WHAT YOU CAN TO HELP
YOU BECAUSE THERE IS GOING TO BE
MASS STARVATION ON LAND.

You as the younger generation have the resources
before you. Do for you because; ALL THE BLING
THAT YOU SEEK WILL MEAN ABSOLUTELY
NOTHING SHORTLY. SHORTLY THE CRY
WILL BE FOOD AND WATER.

Think wise and be wise.

I am seeing. Therefore, I AM IMPLORING YOU TO CHANGE. DO ALL TO SAVE YOU BY PLANTING FOOD, RESERVE AND PRESERVE WATER. GOD IS SHOWING YOU AND TELLING YOU. LISTEN TO GOD. GOD IS NEVER WRONG.

From what I see, ECONOMIES ARE GOING TO FURTHER COLLAPSE. THUS, THE SUPER RICH ARE TRULY NOT THINKING OF ANY OF YOU. THEY'VE SET THEIR FUTURE FOR SUCCESS FOR THEM NOT FAILURE. YOU ARE NOT APART OF THEIR MASTER PLAN.

But in knowing this. They too will fail. All that they do to secure them; their future, their riches, they must fail; lose it all.

Think of your life and future. Right now, it's a foolish man that think all will be safe when all is truly not safe. Think, YOU ARE BLACK. WHO DO YOU THINK WILL BE SAVED FIRST BY WHITE PEOPLE?

So, protect yourself and life from now.

Right now, Black People are on the extinction list. We are not thinking. We are too caught up in their WWW – World Wide Web – Internet.

Now. Go to the movie 40 DAYS AND 40 NIGHTS.

Now tell me.

"HOW MANY BLACK PEOPLE WERE SAVED?"

"WHERE WAS THE FINAL DESTINATION FOR THE RESCUED?"

Go back to your Noah's Ark.

How many were saved here on Earth?

Yes, I see and know the message therefore, I am trying to educate you.

Yes Lovey, NOAH'S ARK IS A POOR EXAMPLE TO USE because; THE BIBLE OF MAN IS A LYING AND NASTY BOOK THEREFORE, TRULY FORGIVE ME BECAUSE; THE STORY OF NOAH IS A CATEGORICAL LIE. YOU

WOULD NEVER PUT CLEAN WITH UNCLEAN PERIOD.

Oh God I truly do not know what the next wave of sickness is going to be and *WHAT DISEASE THESE DISEASED SCIENTIST OF THE GLOBE HAS AND HAVE DEVELOPED TO CAUSE PEOPLE TO ACT LIKE ZOMBIES WHERE THEY HAVE A THIRST FOR BLOOD AND DEATH.*

So, from Eurasia – all of the South Pacific including Hawaii, I truly do not know what is going on and or, what is going to happen to the people. Because of the water; the young man drinking the water, I am not sure if there is RADIATION LEAKAGE SEEPING IN THE WATER IN THE SOUTH PACIFIC DUE TO NUCLEAR STORAGE, BUT SOMETHING IS TRULY NOT RIGHT RIGHT NOW.

I am scared for real.

I do not know why WHITE PEOPLE HAVE TO USE THE LAND OF OTHERS AS THEIR TESTING GROUNDS FOR DEATH; THEIR OWN DIABOLICAL AND

SICK NEEDS WHEN IT COMES TO PLEASING THEIR GOD; DEATH.

No Lovey, WHITE PEOPLE CARE NOT FOR LIFE AND LOOK AT WHAT I AM SEEING NOW.

LOOK AT THE DEATH TOLL THAT IS GOING TO BE ON EARTH BECAUSE OF THEIR SICK/SIKH NATURE.

Yes, I know you showed me them; the White Race as the Sick/Sikh People because they are truly Sick/Sikh.

Lovey, what is wrong with them that they cannot see that their race is dying; hath no place with you due to the evils they do and continue to do here on Earth?

Then after that I had to answer the phone. Apparently, my daughter had gone out and returned and needed to be buzzed into the building. Now I am writing.

It's almost 8pm, and I am going to take my dog for a quick walk and come back; eat, and write. My last child bought me food, and I am truly grateful and thankful for this.

LORD WATCH OVER OUR SHOULDERS by Garnett Silk

However, Lovey, _I REFUSE TO FEED MY ENEMIES BECAUSE; YOU DID NOT TELL ME TO FEED MY ENEMIES._

No Lovey, I cannot feed my enemies. Look at how evil many if not all in the White Race is/are.

Look at how the White Race depict you in their Demonic Book – so-called holy Bible.

No Lovey, I cannot feed my enemies because I know your hurt and pain. Whites has and have done everything to depict you as unclean.

Whites have and has done all to destroy you and others in the NAME OF RELIGION; THEIR RELIGIOUS LIES OF SIN AND UNCLEANLINESS; NASTINESS AS WELL AS, GREED. THEIR THIRST AND GREED TO CONTROL AND DOMINATE THE DIFFERENT LANDS.

No Lovey. Look how they; Whites use Religion to rape and massacre people.

Religion has and have taken billions from life; you Lovey come on now.

No Lovey. It's time people wake up and know that Religion has and have killed them Physically and Spiritually.

You Lovey did not give anyone Religions of Men to give anyone come on now. Thus, <u>WHITES USE YOU LOVEY AS A WEAPON AGAINST THE DIFFERENT NATIONS.</u>

<u>So, no Lovey you cannot forgive the White Race for their wrongs and evils Spiritually or Physically come on now.</u>

They cannot run from what they have done to Nations.

The White Race must be held fully accountable for guilt and wrongs; sins; genocide against humans; all life Spiritually and Physically Lovey.

The White Race can no longer <u>CON THE DIFFERENT NATIONS WITH THEIR LIES AND DECEIT GLOBALLY LOVEY COME ON NOW.</u>

<u>CRAZY BALDHEADS</u> Bob Marley and the Wailers.

AS BLACK PEOPLE WE HAVE TO DO ALL THAT IS GOOD AND TRUE TO STAY ALIVE.

WE HAVE TO; MUST BREAK AWAY FROM THE WHITE MAN'S SYSTEMS OF LIES AND DECEIT.

Lies are truly not called for come on now Lovey.

Therefore, Lovey, you and I must be good and true to us.

Mother Earth must be good and true to life; us Lovey come on now. I need better for her. It's time we Lovey lift up each other good and true.

We must unite for the better good of each other Lovey as well as, the better good of our good and true own, the truly trying to be good, and Mother Earth only.

The White Race have to; must pay for all the atrocities they've done to the different nations *INCLUDING, THE ATROCITIES THEY'VE DONE TO MOTHER EARTH, AND YOU LOVEY.*

MICHELLE

AFRICA UNITE by Robert Nesta Marley aka, Bob Marley

READ THE QUOTES OF MARCUS MOSIAH GARVEY.

We are literally dying and we as a nation are not looking at self, and the way we as Black People are killing our own; each other.

We as Black People are helping our enemies to kill us. See Black on Black Crime, Black Ghettos, Black Gangs, Drug Use, Black Deaths, Black Relationships, Births, and more.

All that is negative we take up. We can no longer BLAME SLAVERY when we of ourselves caused our own slavery.

Yes, I've just pissed many of you off, but we as Black People have to face the reality of our unclean and nasty past.

Think and go back or Black to African Origins – beginning.

How did the devil get into Africa originally?

Yes, I am going to leave you to think until another book. So, stop fuming and continue reading. You are an intelligent being. Use your brain; think because, Africans have not told you or the world the truth of Black Origins.

As Black People, we can no longer live as the defeated.

As Black People, we have to gain back our knowledge.

We have to gain back our Black God.

Without knowledge of God and who we are, we are a doomed race of people.

Without the knowledge and truth of God, how are we going to save ourselves?

As Black People, we need to stop putting our hope and trust in false gods. We need to start doing good for self.

We have to start doing good for each other as a collective of people. _Africa is not saving us therefore, we need to start saving us,_ then we can start saving Africa for those who belong in Africa come on now.

We are dying and going to die further as a race and people. We can stop this mass extinction of Blacks. It is you that must want and need to save you from what's to come.

God did not give Black People Churches.
God did not give Black People lies.

God did not give Black People anything unclean.

It's time Black People start living clean and break away from the different death's we've been given to dishonour us, discredit us, let us live nasty, let us live in dysfunction, let us hate and kill each other, die by, and more.

It's time we as Black People learn to respect self and each other.

<u>*FIRE PON ROME*</u> *by Anthony B.*
It's time Black People take off the shackles and chains that chain us to death, the life of death, the nastiness of death, and more. We need to wakeup and live up because it is going to get worse globally.

Stop dying with Death and start living for life. You need a place with God therefore, <u>*PUT THE NASTINESS OF THE WHITE MAN'S*</u> <u>*BIBLE DOWN AND START LIVING CLEAN.*</u>

GOD DID NOT GIVE ANY IN THE BLACK COMMUNITY ANYTHING NASTY TO LIVE BY. THE WHITE RACE; MEN GAVE BLACK PEOPLE AND THE GLOBAL POPULACE LIES TO LIVE BY AS WELL AS, DIE BY.

Thus, the White Man's Bible that is worldwide.

Religion is worldwide and handed down from parents to children thus, continuing the lies and condemnation of you.

Religion is confusion.
Religion is unclean.

Religion takes you from life Physically and Spiritually.

NOW LOOK.

LOOK AT THE ATROCITIES WHITES HAS AND HAVE DONE TO THE DIFFERENT RACES GLOBALLY IN THE NAME OF RELIGION. NOW TELL ME. IS THIS THE GOD YOU AS BLACK PEOPLE WANT TO CONTINUE TO WORSHIP AND PRAISE, DIE BY, AND WITH?

Why want to die with and alongside your enemies?

THINK.

YES, IT'S TIME EVERY BLACK PERSON LICK OUT PAN AFRICA AND DEMAND AFRICANS TELL THE TRUTH OF BLACK ORIGINS, AND OUR BLACK GOD; CREATOR THAT CREATED IT ALL.

Listen, <u>A WHITE GOD WILL NEVER SAVE BLACK PEOPLE BECAUSE, THE GOD OF WHITES IS DEATH.</u> DEATH CANNOT SAVE YOU. DEATH CAN ONLY KILL YOU, AND I'VE TOLD YOU THIS IN OTHER BOOKS.

<u>THE GOD OF BLACKS IS NOT WHITE.</u>

<u>NO WHITE GOD</u> by Sizzla

RELIGION IS OUR SLAVERY.

RELIGION IS OUR DECAY AS A RACE AND PEOPLE.

THE BIBLE OF MAN DISHONOUR US AS A RACE AND PEOPLE.

THE BIBLE OF MAN DISHONOUR OUR BLACK GOD.

RELIGION – THE RELIGION OF MEN DISHONOUR OUR BLACK GOD.

RELIGION DISHONOUR US AS A RACE AND PEOPLE.

You cannot believe in and accept all that is nasty and unclean and think God is going to save you.

It's time BLACK PEOPLE STOP LOOKING AT WHITES AS OUR SAVIOUR BECAUSE THEY ARE NOT. WHITES ARE OUR TRUE DEATH. Thus, White Death. The way in which the spirit of all who are evil dies.

I've told you in other books.

Spiritual Death is White. So, when you see a White Person, you are actually seeing Spiritual Death. What Spiritual Death look like in the Realm of Death.

Physical Death is Black. So, when you see a Black Rasta whether male or female, you are seeing Physical Death. Yes, the Death Angels who hand your Spirit over to Final Death. *However,* Female Black Death whether she wears dreadlocks, or have her hair braided in Corn Rows. *She's the one to SINK*

LANDS AS WELL AS, WARN AND TAKE THE LIFE OF A SAVED; CHOSEN IF THEY; THAT SAVED AND OR, CHOSEN CONTINUALLY INTERFERE IN THE COURSE OF DEATH.

So yes, all that is happening here on Earth, a Saved and or, the Chosen of Life can stop. HAVE THE POWER TO STOP LITERALLY.

So, absolutely no one can take the COLOUR OF SKIN TO GOD. Our skin colour is a reminder of the DIFFERENT LEVELS OF DEATH.

So, God cannot look at your skin colour. God must; have to look at your "TRUTH," goodness and truth. Thus, humans were told:

"TRUTH IS EVERLASTING LIFE."

It's time Black People put down the lies of religion and all the lies White People have and has instilled in us as well as, brainwashed us in and with.

GOD IS LOVE by Beres Hammond & Popcaan.

Right now. EVIL PEOPLE ARE KILLING US SLOWLY, AND IT'S ONLY GOING TO GET WORSE.

So Black People start waking up because as it is right now. _WE DO NOT HAVE LIFE NOR DO WE HAVE A PLACE AND SPACE WITH GOD._

You are being warned. _HEED THE WARNING OF GOD. WITHOUT US AS A RACE AND PEOPLE NOT UNIFYING, WE WILL NOT BE SAVED, NOR WILL WE MAKE IT IN LIFE._

You have your warning get out of the lands of hell.

Listen, RELIGION WAS GIVEN TO YOU TO KILL YOU AND RELIGION DID KILL MANY IN THE BLACK COMMUNITY.

MANY OF YOU BLACKS THAT GO TO CHURCH ARE THINKING YOU ARE SAVED IN CHRIST. WELL, LET ME TELL YOU THIS MORE THAN CATEGORICALLY IN THIS BOOK. _NOT ONE OF YOU ARE SAVED. GOD KNOWS YOU NOT._

<u>NOT ONE OF YOU HAVE YOUR NAME IN THE BOOK OF LIFE WITH GOD.</u> This I can firmly state without doubt. I know this to be the truth, a fact without doubt. Thus, there are no ands, ifs, or buts about this with God.

Thus, I tell you:

<u>"HELL IS FULL OF BLACK PEOPLE AND RECRUITING MORE."</u>

I saw the headstones – graves of them; many. Wow because as Blacks we have and has forgotten.

I am still seeing. Thus, I see the extinction of us as a race and people. You cannot believe in the lies of the bible and think God is pleased with any of you. God is not pleased.

So, because you believe God is nasty, you preach nastiness when it comes to God, you condemn God; Life, all who do not accept your religious lies and nastiness you condemn, you say the bible is the truth of God, you say Jesus died to save you, and more, <u>GOD CANNOT HAVE ANYTHING TO DO WITH YOU NOR CAN GOD SAVE YOU.</u>

God cannot give nasty. God can only give clean and this we as Black People has and have forgotten.

YOU CANNOT LIVE YOUR LIFE FOR NASTINESS AND THINK GOD IS GOING TO SAVE YOU FROM DEATH; THE LIES YOU BELIEVE IN AND ACCEPT.

So, for the good and true; those who are of life, we need to start the EXODUS.

EXODUS by Robert Nesta Marley aka, Bob Marley.

Listen to Exodus and answer all the questions Bob asked you. We as Black People should know who we are.

We as Black People should know what we can do to save self.

We need to move come on now. GOD IS SAVING US. THEREFORE, WE NEED TO ALLOW GOD TO LEAD US TO THE LAND AND LANDS WE ARE TO BE IN.

WE HAVE TO SAVE SELF COME ON NOW.

WE CAN NO LONGER BE CAPTIVES IN LANDS THAT DON'T LIKE US OR WANT US IN THEIR LAND AND LANDS.

TIME WILL TELL by Robert Nesta Marley aka, Bob Marley

"Jah/God will never give the power to a bald head." So, no matter how *THE WHITE RACE THINK THEY HAVE POWER HERE ON EARTH THEY HAVE ABSOLUTELY NOTHING BECAUSE; TIME IS TELLING FOR THIS RACE.*

All the atrocities they've; the White Race has and have done here on Earth, they; the White Race must account for it and pay for in Hell. The Hell they've created for self.

All the lies they've; the White Race told on God here on Earth, the White Race; all the races must account for; give an account for and pay for in Hell. The Hell they created for self.

Black People, you have the power of God and if you continue to lack unity, Hell is going to consume the lots of you.

I cannot reiterate how God has and have been trying to save us and you are not listening. Time is telling right now.

Earth have to; must get rid of the negatives that plague her. She must purge and or, cleanse herself.

Humans damned near destroyed her and her goodness. It's time for humans to pay; reap the evils they've sown in her come on now.

As for the Children and People of Life, truly make a way home. We have to ensure we have land to plant and harvest clean drinking water.

Know: *THERE MUST BE A MAJOR CONTINENTAL RIFT; SHIFT.* This Earth is gearing up for right now.

PEOPLE GET READY by Curtis Mayfield & the Impressions

Listen to me the Children and People of Life and the Truly Trying to be Good. The train of God is here. We need to get on board right now. Therefore, know that there is no place on board for the wicked and evil of life. Yes, the Sinners of Earth, the Sinners in the grave, the Sinners of the Spiritual Realm, and Beyond, and more. Heed your warning and don't be like the last minute stragglers. Ask God to clearly show you which land you need to be in and do what you can to get there. *Yes, if I had the funds, I would be preparing homes and land space for all of you but at present, many do not know of these books.*

Yes, God knows my truth and true heart therefore, I will forever ever petition God and Mother Earth for the Children and People of Life, and truly trying to be good good and true.

I trust God and Mother Earth to save the true and or, good and true chosen of life.

Mother Earth and God for whom I call Lovey cannot save the Wicked and Evil of Earth or the Spiritual Realm. Evil; all Evil must come to an end.

Therefore, continue praying and seek God as best you can. I know God will make a good way for us all. Yes, I need God to save us by providing for us good and true financially, food wise, water wise, land wise so that we can escape, but all with me and God takes time. So yes, I need you good and true to help me to help you, God, Mother Earth, and all the saved in life.

WAKE UP EVERYBODY by Harold Melvin & The Blue Notes

The truth must be told, and all must tell the truth. Therefore, wakeup and listen. Start telling the truth. Once all is said and done here on Earth, *there is a great storm; tribulation to be had for all that have their name in the Book of Death.* Therefore, I will forever tell you, *LIFE IS NOT JUST PHYSICAL. LIFE IS SPIRITUAL ALSO. And yes, DEATH IS NOT JUST PHYSICAL. DEATH IS SPIRITUAL ALSO.*

Therefore, listen to this song and heed the message and warning of this song.

No one can buy their way into the Realm of God thus, WOE BE UNTO THE RICH AND FOOLISH. Yes, all who think they can bypass Death.

Woe be unto those who have sold their soul for naught; fame and fortune because, there is no place for them in the Realm of Life; God.

Woe be unto those who have accepted the Mark of Death; Beast, because; there is no place for them in the Realm of Life; God.

Doctors of Death, Priests of Death, Politicians of Death, and more. No, let me leave you alone because; I know your hell thus, *YOU ALL NEED TO READ THE BOOK THE NEW BOOK OF KNOWLEDGE BY MICHELLE AND LOVEY; GOD.*

Michelle
June 3, 2021

It's June 4, 2021, and I truly do not know what is going on with Black Lands.

It's weird. I was dreaming about Burkina Faso, and I just now looked on Google for Burkina Faso. What is it with African Countries that Blacks are so clueless, dysfunctional, corrupt, warmongers, hath no life whatsoever, and more?

I truly cannot remember the dream of Burkina Faso, but Lovey, IF YOU WANT BLACK PEOPLE TO GO BACK TO AFRICA, THE DIFFERENT CONFLICTS IN AFRICA MUST CEASE.

AS BLACKS OF THE WESTERN HEMISPHERE, WE CANNOT GO BACK TO AFRICA AND LIVE IN DYSFUNCTION, NOR CAN WE TAKE OUR SLAVE AND BRAINWASHED MENTALITY BACK TO AFRICA WITH US COME ON NOW.

We cannot repeat the past.
Africa cannot receive evil back in her.
Mama Africa cannot give rise again to evil.

She too; Mama Africa have to change for the better good of life.

AS BLACKS WE HAVE TO CHANGE OUR WAY OF THINKING.

WE HAVE TO START THINKING POSITIVE.
WE HAVE TO START BEING POSITIVE PEOPLE.

WE HAVE TO HAVE GOOD AND TRUE LIFE COME ON NOW.

WE HAVE TO STOP OUR WHOREDOM – ALL WHOREDOM COME ON NOW.

LOVEY, WE HAVE TO CHANGE OURSELF.
WE HAVE TO.

WE HAVE TO CHANGE OUR WAY OF EATING.
WE HAVE TO BE UNITED.

WE HAVE TO HAVE GOOD ENTERPRISE AMONGST EACH OTHER.

WE HAVE TO SUPPORT EACH OTHER GOOD AND TRUE.

WE CAN NO LONGER BE SLAVES.

WE CAN NO LONGER BE FOOLS TO THE DIFFERENT NATIONS.

WE CAN NO LONGER SELL OUT OUR LAND AND PEOPLE TO THE HIGHEST BIDDER.

WE CAN NO LONGER LET FOREIGNERS COME INTO OUR LANDS AND ADOPT BLACK CHILDREN. WE AS BLACK PEOPLE HAVE TO TAKE PRIDE IN OURSELF, AND OUR CHILDREN.

WE CAN NO LONGER HAVE CHILDREN WE CANNOT AFFORD TO RAISE GOOD AND TRUE COME ON NOW LOVEY.

WE CAN NO LONGER LIVE IN LIES. WE HAVE TO AND MUST LIVE IN THE TRUTH, AND BY THE TRUTH.

WE HAVE TO CHANGE ALL OUR NEGATIVE WAYS OF DOING THINGS COME ON NOW LOVEY.

WE HAVE TO STOP FAILING SELF AND EACH OTHER.

WE HAVE TO STOP FAILING YOU LOVEY COME ON NOW.

IT'S TIME WE STOP LETTING THE DIFFERENT RACES INCLUDING OUR OWN SACRIFICE US TO DEATH.

IT'S TIME WE STOP SELLING OURSELF SHORT.

WE HAVE TO STOP SELLING OUR LANDS SHORT.

WE HAVE TO CLEAN; MUST CLEAN OURSELF NOW LOVEY COME ON NOW.

AFRICA AND AFRICANS MUST CLEAN UP THE CONTINENT BECAUSE AS IT IS, I KNOW FOR A FACT WITHOUT DOUBT THAT ALL OF AFRICA WILL NOT BE SAVED; CANNOT BE SAVED COME ON NOW.

Now Lovey, hear me and truly listen to me now because; *this is an irrevocable demand; need on my part* with You, Me, Mother Earth, all that is Good and True, the Universe, The Sun and Moon, and yes, more good and true things.

This irrevocable demand; need on my part has to do with the dream I had this morning.

Dreamt water; Your Blessings coming down Lovey and people had their feet out as water came down on their feet. People had their shoes off their feet. In the dream, you could not see the faces of the people, only the lower part of their feet. Now dis one dutty crebbay crebbay one with white feet had her black shoe on. Yes, female shoes.

Now Lovey, I should be pissed, and in a way I am pissed but; I am going to curve my anger because; *IF I CUSS OUT THE WHITE RACE IN THIS BOOK EVEN YOU WOULD QUINGE TO HOW I WOULD GO OFF ON THIS NASTY RACE OF DEMONS THAT THINK LIFE IS A JOKE, AND YOUR OFFERING AND BLESSING IS A JOKE LOVEY. THUS, TRULY HEAR ME AND ACT ON MY REQUEST BECAUSE IT IS TRULY NEEDED.*

I am not having it with White People anymore. I am truly fed up of them and their arrogance.

Yes, the different nations can hate my ass but bun dem. I will not give you up for anyone in this world or anywhere Lovey. You are not a joke, and I cannot have nasty white people dirty us, our life, our path, our right and rights, our world, and more with you ever again. *I CATEGORICALLY REFUSE NASTY WHITE PEOPLE. Dyam wrenk dem bi.*

Remember you asked me to WRITE YOU A BOOK AND I AM WRITING. THIS IS JUST ONE OF THE MANY BOOKS I'VE WRITTEN YOU THEREFORE, BECAUSE YOU HAVE ASKED ME TO WRITE YOU A BOOK, AND I HAVE BEEN DOING SO, I NEED YOU TO LOOK INTO MY

REQUESTS AND GRANT THEM ESPECIALLY WHAT I AM GOING TO ASK OF YOU NOW.

HAVE NO REGRETS.

MOTHER EARTH HAVE NOT REGRETS.

I WILL HAVE NO REGRETS LOVEY BECAUSE YOU ARE MY GOOD AND TRUE HOPE AND CHOICE FOR LIFE AND IN LIFE. I CANNOT LET THE WHITE RACE DIRTY ALL WE ARE TRYING TO ACHIEVE HERE ON EARTH THEREFORE, MY REQUEST MUST BE IRREVOCABLE MORE THAN FOREVER EVER WITHOUT END CONTINUALLY WITHOUT END.

BECAUSE OF DI DUTTY BITCH WITH HAR SHOE ON, YOU HAVE TO NOW WALK AWAY FULLY AND TRUTHFULLY FROM THE WHITE RACE. THIS WALKING AWAY MUST BE IRREVOCABLE MORE THAN FOREVER EVER WITHOUT END MORE THAN CONTINUALLY WITHOUT END. I AM TIRED OF THIS RACE DIRTYING OUR BLESSINGS HERE ON EARTH. THEREFORE, _YOUR LOCKING OUT OF THE OF THE WHITE RACE HERE ON EARTH AND THE SPIRITUAL REALM MUST BE MORE THAN IRREVOCABLE WITHOUT END MORE THAN CONTINUALLY WITHOUT END._

YOU LOVEY CANNOT BE SHOWERING US WITH YOUR BLESSINGS – WATER AND DEM – DIS DUTTY WRETCH HAVE HAR BLACK SHOE PON HAR FOOT. NO, THAT IS BIG TIME DISRESPECT COME ON NOW. SO YES, IT GOES TO SHOW YOU THAT WHITE PEOPLE; YES, NOT ALL WILL FOREVER EVER DISRESPECT LIFE; YOU LOVEY COME ON NOW. Yes, all the feet in the dream were white but dis one had to show her disrespect.

No Lovey, I cannot have White People disrespecting you, your blessings, your life, and more. White People don't want true life, truly leave them the hell alone. Do not bother with this race of demons.

The Bible of Man; them, the White Race is a testament of how evil they are therefore, leave them the hell alone. *YOU CANNOT BLESS PEOPLE THAT CONTINUALLY DISRESPECT YOU, BLACK PEOPLE, MOTHER EARTH; ALL LIFE FOR THAT MATTER COME ON NOW.*

So yes, the LOCK OUT OF WHITE PEOPLE FROM THE REALM OF TRUTH AND LIFE MUST BE IRREVOCABLE MORE THAN FOREVER EVER MORE THAN CONTINUALLY

WITHOUT END. THUS, THIS RACE CAN NEVER EVER FIND LIFE IN YOU LOVEY. I HAVE TO PETITION YOU FOR THIS. YES, HARSH BUT IT MUST BE THIS WAY.

I HAVE TO BE HARSH BECAUSE IN FULL TRUTH, I TRULY DO NOT WANT OR NEED ANYMORE EVIL ON EARTH. WE CANNOT AFFORD TO BRING BACK ANY FORM OF EVIL, STRIFE, DISRESPECT, DISUNITY, SIN, AND MORE EVIL AND NEGATIVE THINGS BACK TO EARTH. WE HAVE TO PROTECT SELF AND EARTH LOVEY COME ON NOW.

You have the strength and power to grant my true desire therefore, let it be Lovey. Look into what I am saying.

And Lovey, this irrevocable request goes for all the Blacks that fall under the White Banner of Death no matter living or dead. I cannot have NASTY BLACK PEOPLE BRINGING BACK EVIL INTO EARTH ONCE ALL EVIL IS GONE. I will not be defeated by my own Blacks Lovey. I refuse to be.

"It should not take Death to unify Blacks Lovey."

"It should not take DEATH TO CLEARLY STATE BLACKS LACK UNITY LOVEY."

Look into my dream Lovey.
Look into what I saw.

Find justice and or, good favour in my asking and ensure we are truly saved. We have to protect ourself from all facets of evil come on now.

Life is truly worth it for us and our good and true own come on now. Like I said, I will not stand anyone disrespecting you. Let them go period.

You need to protect you Lovey from those who truly hate you.

You need to protect the good and true from those who truly hate you Lovey as well as, will now hate us; the good and true.

You are my true Love Lovey, and I will defend you with every fabric of my being. It's time you Lovey see yourself good and true in life and stop trying to save people that truly hate you, or don't want to be saved.

IT'S TIME MOTHER EARTH SUPPORT YOU LOVEY IN GOODNESS AND IN TRUTH.

MOTHER EARTH HAVE TO RESPECT YOU AND LIFE AND SHUT DOWN ALL EVIL THAT IS WITHIN HER. SHE HAVE TO; MUST SIFT AWAY FROM EVIL LANDS. SHE CANNOT ACCOMMODATE EVIL LANDS COME ON NOW.

IT'S TIME MOTHER EARTH LET GO ALL FACETS OF EVIL WITHIN HER AND AROUND HER.

IT'S TIME MOTHER EARTH RESPECT HERSELF GOOD AND TRUE.

IT'S TIME MOTHER EARTH ADHERE TO THE GOODNESS AND TRUTH OF LIFE.

IT'S TIME MOTHER EARTH LET GO OF DESTRUCTIVE HUMANS. SHE CAN NO LONGER SUPPORT EVIL FOOD WISE, AND WATER WISE LOVEY AND NEITHER CAN YOU LOVEY COME ON NOW.

How much more should I talk to you Lovey for you to look into things and do all the good and true you can do for yourself, the good and true of life, and truly trying to be good only?

We can no longer let Death and the Children and People of Death be dependent on us for life anymore. Life cannot give rise to death therefore, Death should not look to us to sustain and maintain the Children and People of Death.

Female Black Death freaks when the Chosen and or, a Chosen interfere in the Course of Death. Now, I am complaining Lovey. Death must go with their wicked and evil own and stop interfering with the good and true life of the good and true, and truly trying to be good. All who seek to hurt the good and true; Death should deal with them according to the Law and Laws of Death period.

Therefore Lovey, <u>OUR GOODNESS CANNOT GO TO SUSTAINING AND MAINTAINING THE WHITE RACE ANYMORE. IT'S TIME TO TRULY LET THIS RACE; THE WHITE RACE GO.</u>

<u>LOVEY, THEY CANNOT CLING TO THE BLACK RACE ANYMORE EITHER. THEREFORE, ALL WHO BELONG TO DEATH IN THE WHITE RACE MUST GO FROM LIFE. LIFE CAN NO LONGER SUPPORT THEM.</u>

LIFE CAN NO LONGER MAINTAIN AND SUSTAIN THEM.

LIFE CAN NO LONGER FEED THEM.
LIFE CAN NO LONGER WATER THEM.
LIFE CAN NO LONGER MARRY THEM.

LIFE CAN NO LONGER HAVE COMPASSION ON THEM OR FOR THEM.

LET THEM GO LOVEY. JUST AS THE LOCKOUT OF ALL OF BABYLON WAS AND IS STILL IRREVOCABLE UNTIL THIS DAY, THE LOCKOUT OF ALL IN THE WHITE RACE MUST BE IRREVOCABLE ALSO.

Now this other dream. I do not know how to make sense of Lovey. This dream had to do with a Black Land it seems. There was this lady, Older Black Lady that I would say in her late fifties and or, early sixties. This Black Man was beside her. They knew each other. His son was with them. His son was a mixture of Black and Indian – Babylonian Indian but, he looked more Indian than Black and or, Mixed.

Apparently, a news reporter was interviewing them, but you did not see the news reporter. The Black Man said to the elder Black Lady he wanted to marry her, and she told him he could not handle her. Plus, she was married to someone.

But Lovey, what struck me was the _BLACKNESS OF LAND THAT WAS BEHIND THEM THAT THEY COULD NOT SEE. IT WAS AS IF THE LAND WAS CHARRED; UPROOTED IN DARKNESS; BLACKNESS TO HOW BLACK AND HILLY THE SOIL WAS._ It was like Lava had left its mark on the land.

Now, I do not know what is going to happen in the Caribbean destruction wise apart from what is happening in St. Vincent and the Grenadines.

I so do not know what land is going to get devastated because I don't think these people were Jamaicans. So, from Guyana, Suriname, all of the Caribbean including, Trinidad and Tobago, and I am going to extend it to Brazil, Belize, Mexico, and more. People need to be on the alert. Keep in mind that destruction is going to happen more and more on land.

So yes, I am dreaming about the destruction of Black People Globally. Not every Black Land will be saved because, I know MANY BLACK LANDS AND PEOPLE FALL UNDER THE ORDER OF

DEATH; WHITE DEATH. Thus, many Blacks must go down with Death.

Now Lovey, please heed this as well when it comes to Black People. And I know I talked about this in other books.

THOSE BLACK PEOPLE THAT REFUSE TO LISTEN TO YOUR CALL WHICH IS OUR GOOD AND TRUE CALL, TRULY WALK AWAY FROM THESE BLACKS. HAVE ABSOLUTELY NOTHING TO DO WITH THEM BECAUSE ONCE AGAIN BLACKS WOULD HAVE PROVEN TO YOU MORE THAN CATEGORICALLY THAT THEY'VE CHOSEN DEATH OVER LIFE.

THEY ARE WAITING FOR DEATH; THEIR JESUS TO SAVE THEM. So, truly leave them alone. And I know you've left them alone.

NO LOVEY, I WILL NOT TOLERATE DISOBEDIENCE ANYMORE WHEN IT COMES TO BLACK PEOPLE.

YOU KNOW MANY WILL DO ALL TO PROVE ME WRONG, FALSE, A LIAR, A FRAUD, AND MORE.

MANY WILL SEEK TO KILL ME.

MANY WILL SEEK TO SET ME UP.

ALL THIS WE KNOW THUS, _AMBUSH IN THE NIGHT_ by Rob Marley and the Wailers. None listened to the different messages he came with and gave to the Black Populace Globally.

So now when them come Lovey with everything to hurt and kill me, I am hoping you turn all back on them more than full throttle. I will not stand with ignorant and stupid Black People that want to die with Death.

LIFE CANNOT AND CAN NO LONGER STAND WITH DEATH AND THE CHILDREN AND PEOPLE OF DEATH LOVEY.

THEREFORE, WHEN ALL BLACKS NO MATTER WHERE THEY ARE IN THE WORLD REFUSE TO ACCEPT THE TRUTH OF LIFE YOU LOVEY BY CONTINUING TO SIDE WITH THE DEVIL AND THE CHURCHES OF THE DEVIL, LET THEM BE LIKE UNTO THE WHITE RACE RIGHT THERE AND THEN. LET THEM; BLACKS BE BOUND TO THE GOD AND GODS THEY CHOSE AND CHOOSE AS WELL AS, CONTINUE TO CHOOSE AND CHOSE TO KILL THEM.

MEANING, ALL WHO ARE IN THE DIFFERENT CHURCHES THAT PREACH AND TEACH AGAINST ME, TELL PEOPLE TO BOYCOTT ME, DO ALL MANNER OF EVIL TO ME LET THEM BE BOUND TO HELL; THEREFORE, IRREVOKING LIFE WITH YOU LOVEY.

THEY CANNOT HAVE LIFE WITH YOU BECAUSE THE DECISION TO STAY WITH DEATH IS NOW IRREVOCABLE MORE THAN CONTINUALLY WITHOUT END MORE THAN FOREVER EVER WITHOUT END.

I CANNOT ANYMORE WITH BLACK PEOPLE LOVEY.

I CANNOT STAND TO SEE YOU TRYING TO SAVE US AND WE CONTINUALLY REFUSE YOUR SAVING. SO, THE GOD THEY CHOOSE LET BLACKS BE BOUND TO THAT GOD.

AND LOVEY, IF I HAVE EXPLAINED REVOKING WRONG WHEN IT COMES TO BLACK PEOPLE, DO FORGIVE ME AND CORRECT MY WORDING.

It's time for Blacks to wake up and know the truth Lovey.

Those Blacks that have and has chosen Death for self and family, let them now know that they have no saving grace in you Lovey.

There is no life in death Lovey. All there is is death come on now.

YOU HAVE ABSOLUTELY NOTHING TO DO WITH THE DIFFERENT CHURCHES THEREFORE, YOUR WALKING AWAY FROM PEOPLE IN THE DIFFERENT CHURCHES GLOBALLY MUST ALSO BE IRREVOCABLE MORE THAN FOREVER EVER WITHOUT END CONTINUALLY WITHOUT END.

WE LOVEY CANNOT LOOK BACK ON THE PEOPLE OF DEATH THAT SPREAD LIES ABOUT LIFE.

WE LOVEY CANNOT LOOK BACK ON THE PEOPLE OF DEATH WHO TEACH LIES IN THE NAME OF RELIGION; DEATH.

There is a life to be had Lovey, and we must protect Life from those who truly do now want or need life. _We have to move on._

My choice is right for good and true life therefore, it all must end now for the wicked and evil. You cannot extend the Olive Branch Lovey to the wicked and evil of Earth anymore. I did make the right choice for good and true life here on Earth, in the Spiritual Realm, in the Universe, and Beyond for good and true life that is ever growing good and true continually without end.

I cannot choose Death for our good and true people Lovey. I have to choose good and true life for which I did.

Evil cannot continue to move forward Lovey.

Evil cannot come with us.
Evil must stop.

The destruction of Earth by evil must stop.
The destruction of Blacks must stop.

Black People must stop killing Blacks.

Black People must stop and walk away from the Web of Lies we are caught up in by the different races including, our own.

BABYLON SYSTEM by Bob Marley and the Wailers.

Lovey, we can no longer wail; cry to you Lovey for Black People Globally to wake up from the deep and deadly sleep they are in. I refuse to make provisions of any kind for evil.

Look at Mother Earth Lovey and tell me how good and true are humans to her?

Look at you Lovey and tell me, how good and true humans are to you?

Mother Earth sustain and maintain us, now look at how humans have and has destroyed her.

Look at You Lovey and how the White Race of Demons have and has tried to destroy you with Religion and their Demonic Book – Man's so-called Holy Bible.

Life has always been just and fair, it is humans that cannot be just, or fair Lovey come on now.

So yes, it all ends now Lovey come on now.

If Black People want and need life with you, LET BLACKS COME BACK TO YOU GOOD AND TRUE.

No Lovey. _LEARN FROM MY MISTAKE WITH MY DAUGHTER._

ONCE YOU LET GO OF A RACE AND PEOPLE, DON'T EVER WANT THEM BACK NO MATTER HOW HARD THEY TRY BECAUSE; DESPITE THEIR BEGGING AND TEARS; THEIR EVIL AND DIRTY HEART CANNOT CHANGE. I LEARNT THIS THE HARD WAY. THEREFORE, I WILL FOREVER EVER SAY:

"DUTTY CAANE COME CLEAN."

"DIRTY WILL ALWAYS BE DIRTY."

YOU KNOW THIS AS WELL LOVEY BECAUSE YOU SHOWED ME THIS. Yes, it's a painful lesson we have to learn hence we have to learn it.

Going back to your blessing and the white foot with the black shoe. You are showing me that despite your goodness and truth towards the White Race they will forever dirty life.

We cannot let the White Race or any race or anyone for that matter dirty Earth and Us ever again Lovey come on now. We cannot save people who truly do not want or need saving.

It's time we protect our good and true own and I cannot state this anymore with you Lovey. _RIGHT NOW, BLACK PEOPLE CANNOT SEE THEIR OWN DEATH. I SEE IT AND I AM TELLING THEM, BUT HOW MANY WILL LISTEN?_

HOW MANY WILL ADHERE TO GOOD AND TRUE COUNSEL; TEACHING?

HOW MANY WILL CHANGE THEIR DIRTY WAYS?

HOW MANY WILL COME BACK TO YOU LOVEY CLEAN AND TRUE?

HOW MANY WILL DO THE GOOD THEY CAN TO SAVE THEIR GOOD AND TRUE OWN?

IT'S OVER FOR BILLIONS LOVEY. LET IT STAY OVER FOR BILLIONS LOVEY COME ON NOW.

Going back to my Zombie Dream yesterday. Humans truly do not know what is going to fully happen on Earth. Everyone is so wrapped up in Social Media; getting likes, being seen, selling self, selling lies, going viral, and more that they cannot see that the extinction of humans is inevitable for billions. NONE IS TRYING TO SAVE SELF. They are too preoccupied with their Social Status Globally.

Remember in my earlier books Lovey I said, *"the MENU IS GOING TO READ NOW SERVING HUMANS."* Well, we are getting down to that state.

Well, you do have people eating people; the flesh and or, carcass of humans already literally. It is going to get worse shortly.

Yes, I know not all in the Black Race can be saved and will not be saved, but I cannot and will not worry about these Blacks. The choice of life was not their stay, focus, and truth.

I have to think of us Lovey and the good and true including, truly trying to be good only. These people we need to prepare for. So, as I close this book in goodness and in truth, please clearly outline the lands you need our good and true people and the truly trying to migrate to on a map.

I know Africa is a place for us to go to, but which lands because; I truly do not want or need any of our people in Sudan, Ethiopia, Eretria, Somalia, Iraq, Iran, Israel, and more lands Lovey.

I need you to be our good and true guide to take us truly and truthfully home. Yes, not to be disrespectful and I won't. I truly do not need you to be our Moses. I need you to be our good and true guide, all, protector, strength, all we need to come home to you good and true.

Yes, I need Mother Earth to now help us by changing the content of her soil to be good and true, fertile, easy to till, truly balanced for us only Lovey; the good and true, and truly trying to be good. Our waterways must now be the waterways of the wicked and evil Lovey. Not even a tat of water I give to the wicked and evil no matter how they cry out for need and mercy. All that the wicked and evil try to do to us Lovey must fail.

Therefore, the evil of evil must now fully and truly return to evil without delay. I refuse to share my space and life with you Lovey beside, amongst, or with any form of evil. You know this. Therefore, we truly need each other.

We have to support each other.

We have to truly give to each other.
We have to be truly there for each other.
We have to protect each other.

Yes Lovey, we need to clean together.

So yes, Black People. This book is our wake up call to start changing; unifying in order to save us truthfully and good.

And yes, if you feel this book is incomplete, I feel the same way.

Michelle

It's June 6, 2021 in the afternoon, and I had myself a beautiful sleep. I took my dog very early this morning for a walk. Had breakfast, wrote, played a bit of games then went back to sleep.

Dreamt of game play; my game play which is fine. At times my game play here in the Physical do spill over in my dream world.

Yes, my irrevocable demand and want spilt over in my dream world as well because; I was talking to about this in my dream world.

I will not stand down from this request of God because _humans need a wake up call in regards to Religion and using God, and the name of God as their weapon to rape, kill, rip families apart, and more evil things._ God need to address this as well, and truly walk away from the demons that profess to be holy. The world; people of the world need to turn against these monsters of Religion and Religion itself that rip Life from Life Physically and Spiritually. Thus, the book; _THE NEW BOOK OF KNOWLEDGE BY MICHELLE AND LOVEY; GOD._ God need to ensure all that is written Penalty Wise, and more come to fruition for the Wicked and Evil of Life here on Earth and in the

Spiritual Realm. Evil cannot get away with the atrocities they've done here on Earth in the name of God, and more.

Do not use God to deceive and lie to nations. Unnu an Gad anno size.

Dyam stink an wrenk unnu bi. Thus, <u>NO RELIGION IS OF GOD, AND WOE TO ALL WHO ARE OF AND IN RELIGION GLOBALLY.</u>

Further, humans need to realize that ONCE YOU ACCEPT UNCLEAN IN YOUR LIFE, YOU CANNOT LIVE CLEAN. YOU HAVE TO LIVE DIRTY, and humans are living dirty.

Now, not too long ago I dreamt this BLACK OBEAH WOMAN. She had her wrap head, and she was dressed in Blue. At the gate – one of the opening that led to the building I live in. East opening. She had planted something in the ground, and it killed this man; older man. I did not see the man's face. The man did die and now she was taking up what she planted in the ground that killed him.

Now, I was walking on the side walk and she was coming towards my direction planting things in the ground. The fence separated us. Now I am listening to:

LION PAW by Tarrus Riley.

I know I can listen to NO WEAPON by Fred Hammond, but I am going to keep Lion Paw without the Selassie because; this song truly tells how some in the Black Community are nasty. Thus, they rely on Obeah, Voodoo, _Science_ to kill and get what they want.

So yes, many in the Black Race walk with Demons, and do the bidding of Demons.

Bitch mi noa yu. I know you killed him.

I know, I know, I know therefore, you have some BLACK WOMEN OUT THERE THAT ARE MORE THAN NASTY AND DISGUSTING.

No Lovey, I know the use of Obeah but to use Obeah to kill your husband. You're a BC Demon. That is premeditated murder Lovey come on now.

So, no matter unnu obeah, mi a si.

Further, apart from the Obeah, I know Ontario is going to be hit by destruction because; she was planting something in the ground after taking up the nastiness of what she did to him. Just what that destruction is, I have to watch and see. Yes, the grass was green, but I cannot tell of the destruction that will happen in Ontario; if we are going to have a Earthquake, storm, flooding. I just have to watch and see.

Yes, I did feel the Earth Vibrating for which I told you about at the beginning of this book. So yes, maybe this Obeah Woman is confirming that Ontario is going to have an Earthquake. The magnitude of the Quake I truly do not know.

Michelle.

BOOKS WRITTEN BY MICHELLE JEAN 2021

MY TALK JANUARY 2021

MY TALK JANUARY 2021 – BOOK TWO

MINI BOOK

JUST TALKING – THINKING

A LITTLE TALK WITH MOTHER EARTH

I NEED ANSWERS GOD

POETRY MY WAY

THE MIND AND SPIRITUALITY

I NEED ANSWERS GOD – PART TWO

MY NIGHTS

I NEED ANSWERS GOD – PART THREE

GOD IS GOOD

WHAT ABOUT US

WOW WHAT

AFRICAN – BLACK PEOPLE CUSS OUT